The Bay of Lost Love

Victoria Sedova

I0808421

BookLand press

Copyright © 2012 by Victoria Sedova

All rights reserved. No part of this publication may be reproduced or transmitted in any form or by any means, electronic or mechanical, including photocopying, recording, or any information storage and retrieval, without the written permission of the publisher.

Names, characters, places and incidents are either the product of the author's imagination or used fictitiously, and any resemblance to actual persons living or dead, events or locales is entirely coincidental. All trademarks are properties of their respective owners.

Published by BookLand Press
15 Allstate Parkway, Suite 600, Markham, Ontario L3R 5B4
www.booklandpress.com

Printed and bound in Canada.

Library and Archives Canada Cataloguing in Publication

Sedova, Victoria
The bay of lost love / Victoria Sedova.

Poems.
ISBN 978-1-926956-34-3

I. Title.

PS8637.E436B39 2012 C811'.6 C2012-906259-6

Canada Council for the Arts Conseil des arts du Canada

ONTARIO ARTS COUNCIL
CONSEIL DES ARTS DE L'ONTARIO

We acknowledge the support of the Canada Council for the Arts, which last year invested $154 million to bring the arts to Canadians throughout the country. We acknowledge the support of the Ontario Arts Council (OAC), an agency of the Government of Ontario, which last year funded 1,681 individual artists and 1,125 organizations in 216 communities across Ontario for a total of $52.8 million. We acknowledge the financial support of the Ontario Media Development Corporation for our publishing activities.

Dedicated to my husband,
who is always there for me
through good times and bad times

"And now here is my secret, a very simple secret; it is only with the heart that one can see rightly, what is essential is invisible to the eye."

~ *Antoine de Saint Exupéry*

Table of Contents

For You | 11

Stars | 12

Think of Me | 13

I Will Bewitch You | 14

My World | 15

I Am | 16

The Love | 17

The Offer | 18

Visit | 19

Two Lives | 20

She-Wolf | 21

He and She | 22

Two Strangers | 23

Phantom of Love | 24

At Night | 25

Moonlight | 26

The First Snowfall | 27

Angel | 28

Talking to Death | 29

I Ask the Darkness | 30
The Riddle | 31
Too Late | 32
Conversation | 33
One Day | 34
Nostalgia | 35
Wedding Thoughts | 36
Lonely | 37
I Asked the Boy | 38
Bride | 39
Promise | 40
Confession | 41
Don't Calm Me | 42
The Ache | 43
Rain in the City | 44
Trembling Hand | 45
Wind | 46
The Autumn Is a Thief | 47
Separation | 48
Don't Let Me Go | 49
The End | 50
You Left | 51
Forget About Me | 52
Set Me Free | 53
Forgive Me | 54

Farewell | 55

Without You | 56

I Wouldn't | 57

That Wasn't Love | 58

It's Over | 59

Mistake | 60

Forever | 61

Leave Everything Behind | 62

Life Story | 63

Love Dies | 64

If You Remember | 65

You Are Somewhere | 66

The Star | 67

Letters | 68

The Love Is Gone | 69

The Bay of Lost Love | 70

For You

For you I will become the night
Embrace you in the gentle darkness
I'll keep tranquillity until the morning
And then for you I will become the sun
Light up your way all busy day until the dusk
For you I will become the sea
And slowly play with you
With kissing rocking waves
For you I will become the witch
And cast the spells, conquer a dragon
For you I could be all but you want nothing

Stars

The night as veil has covered sleeping city
The wind stopped howling to respect the night
I looked at sky and heard your gentle whispers
Each other interrupting all the time
The shining stars were talking
Illuminating sleeping universe
I saw for an instant stars as living beings
Which only come to sight at night
And quickly hide behind the playful clouds
There is no coincidence in stars' alignment
They form the constellations for a reason
Concealing answers to all forbidden themes
But being far away from earth
The stars don't know rules of nature
The laws and meaning of the love
Through depths of time and years
The stars observe us willing to
Accept the human soul as another star
Sometimes the careless star is
Overcoming distance and pays the visit
Granting treasured wish
I saw another shooting star was coming
What should I ask when making a wish?
Maybe I'll ask for love or maybe for forgiveness
Wait, no I'll ask to be a star
A falling star for you to make your wish come true

Think of Me

Think of me in winter morning
When angry blizzard knocking at the door
Think of me in placid day of spring
When lazy streams are flowing idly
Think of me in starry summer night
When moon is astonishingly bright
Think of me in autumn evening
When wind is chasing heavy clouds
Think of me to keep flame burning
I am always near... think of me

I Will Bewitch You

I will bewitch you
I will light red candle
Mix herbs and add
Some heavy brew
Pour in the silver chalice
I'll cast my spell for love
It will be on for ages
I'll become your
Day and night
And you'll be
My wicked knight
You'll come to me
Or else you wouldn't live
I'll be your pleasure
Your grief
Unruly wind had
Own plans and
Blew my candle
And broke my spell
I couldn't charm you
But I will wait for you
And you will come
Or else I wouldn't live

My World

My world is weaved from eccentric dreams
My world is vivid, immature and stunning
My world is a bewitching endless garden
With talking trees and singing crystal pond
With sun and moon living in the same house
With poet-cat and book critiquing mouse

I Am

I am the woman - time without end
I am the magic star - the mystery unsolved
I am eternity - I cannot die or be reborn
I am the sun - will shine or vanish in the clouds
I'll rise from the ashes and conquer the world
For you, but your motto is
"I don't need the world when I'm bored"

The Love

The love is a furious wave
The love is a violent torrent
The love is a poisonous plant

The love is a screeching of eagles
The love is a storm and squall
The love is malicious trouble

The love is an envy and spite
The love is last day of the life
The love is the sun and the rain

The love is seclusion and shelter
The love is a treacherous fight
The love is a skydiving flight

The love is a grief and anguish
The love is inferno and blaze
The love is amazing grace

The Offer

I offered you the ocean of pleasure
You offered me the whirlwind in return

I offered you infinite reliance
You offered hesitation in return

I offered you my everlasting soul
You brought me evil spirit in return

I offered fondness, tender and passion
You offered me aversion in return

I offered you my heart
Do not be shy and crush it in return

Visit

When day will grow dim
I'll enter in your soul on my tiptoes
And open the doors
Don't rush me, don't object it
I'll bring the fortune or distress
Depends on luck
These days I dream of love
Of future, of beloved
I wish to be with you
All night and light a candle
You saying this is wrong time
And I'm no longer welcome
I grew accustomed to your room
To pictures in the golden frames
To gramophone with autumn songs of rains
To rustling leaves on time-worn floor
And chest with letters which you wrote
But never mailed - I waited so long
Ridiculous... you know
We cannot domineer the stars
To change the planets' course
Forget about talk and bring wine glasses
And pour the love but don't add the insult
We drank too much the wine of separation
Today we'll light extinguished star and talk all night
Before falling down into the abyss

Two Lives

The love will never understand
The "no" word and its meaning
The pangs of loss and the seclusion
The love is wise, it is old as universe
The love is always coming sudden
As summer thunderstorm
Love needs just one confession
Love cannot be on hold or waiting list
It comes and goes as it pleases
And links two lives in one
Fantastic foolish disappointment

She-Wolf

She never felt the fear
Walking through the crowd
She searched for somebody
For traces, for the whiff
Familiar to her of nowhere
She listened only call of heat
Avoiding haunting strangers
Was ready to fight the unforeseen
Escaped from enemies without losing faith
She treasured love in her wolf's spirit
She missed him greatly, sometimes very loud
And creepy chill crawled under people's skin
In those who could hear she-wolf grieving
She was an extraordinary wolf
Unlike the other species
She looked in human eyes and saw his love
She thought she found him but all that time
The sneaky destiny bewildered pages
Of oldest book - the Book of Love

He and She

He had the talent to compose verses
Reviving causality of thoughts
She had the talent to give an absolution
Curing disadvantaged with the words
He was a temerarious gambler
And played without estimating price
She had a gift to love ardently
Her feelings could've melt the arctic ice
He rushed to light ravenous fires
Ignoring warnings from all-seeing stars
She flipped through long days and waited
Regretting life and passing time

Two Strangers

Two strangers met online at random
First stranger - very sad and sought advice
Another stranger was more cheerful
But had a lot of trouble finding love
They had discussions with each other
They built a friendship and
Learned about personalities a lot
First stranger put behind his sadness
And found kindness and support
Another stranger fell in love
Without even noticing, but kept a secret
He couldn't find right words
They talked all nights until the dawn
And were happy
The days flew by and then there was
The question from first stranger:
When should we meet?
The second stranger panicked
And deleted all his words and hopes
Because he fell in love with phantom

Phantom of Love

I only want to touch you but you are the air
You are neophyte from a different world
You don't understand me
At least you can hear my words streaming away

I'm looking at you in the old garbled mirror
The image deceives me and moving away
You are teasing the silence and spinning my hope
I'm using sweet lies to patch my sadness

I'm holding phantom in insensible hands
I'm drinking the poisonous honey
The image fading in silvery haze
And suddenly vanished leaving me shattered

My broken heart stops beating
I'm passing away and I'm leaving the earth
Cheating death, flying through the universe
I am in different world now
I'll be your neophyte

At Night

My soul is boundless at night
You are appearing from the darkness
And then the sudden sun is rising
And holding agonizing light

I only live at night
Past carries me away in deep abyss
Of faded lovely years of life
When you were with me

The sun is beaming youthful smile
Entwine the pearls of dew into the morning
The mistress night is leaving as a silent shade
Without touching us, ignoring

Your embrace and warmth
Are so light and so seductive
The dreams are slithered by
The night is breathing hard

New day is coming once again
Returning me into the present
Somewhere in my dreams
You are unchanged again
As during faded awful years

Moonlight

Moonlight is peeking through the window
Seducing me with ice cold golden paint
Bringing quaint dreams and memories
As in eerie fairy game
I dissect my black mind luring heavens
I return to you all my regrets
Darkness took me, keeping secrets
Sending to the unsuspecting earth
Fleet of revengeful corvettes
Made from moonlight tears and stardust
Soothing scorching fire, your fears
Libel words and wings of ghastly dreams

The First Snowfall

Here's winter, the first snowfall
Pristine, captivating and pure
Snowfall is hiding the trace
Of all what we've done with existence

I already have nothing to ask
You or destiny, ominous heavens
I will bury the pain in the darkest
Corner of heart and will drop
In the snow to make snow angels

You'd remember the spring
Snow white blossom was
Like today's snowfall quickly
Passed crazy spring and
Brought nothing but indecision

Now I'll leave my body to freeze
The first snow will render a favour
The first snow: pristine, captivating and pure
The first snow
My only saviour

Angel

Bogged down in the seething blizzard
On winter streets forgotten by the spring
White angel wandered in the crowd
With slow bleeding fractured wing

All people hastened through the evening
Preoccupied with their thoughts
White angel inconspicuous by anybody
Clung to the silent freezing city walls

Ice-covered, shivering from merciless winter
Pushed down by some stranger's hand
He smiled and looked at human souls
To look for kindness and goodwill

The angel looked like a wondrous creature
That visits us from blissful Christmas dreams
Like gem in rough in dirty grimy snow
Like desolated holly on a noisy street

The restless snow continued falling
The ruthless wind sung never-ending song
Ignored by one and all, white angel wafted
Accepting death - the strongest of us all

Talking to Death

On winter coolly gleaming snow
I'm writing words that coming from my heart
And name is still alive and soul
The stars and moon are watching
My invocation to the death
Today I'm throwing challenge
Impudent dare to bring him back
I'll scream and beg: return, you know
Without him I wouldn't live
The trembling voice will fade from lips
I want him back, you see my heart is dying
I'll brush away the freezing tears from cheek
And something sharp in hand will flicker
So you are stubborn, now watch: one cut
In scarlet spotless snow painted
The heart beats slow and fainted
And soon two hearts will be united
Look, death, it cannot be undone
Learn what a woman can accomplish
When you will dare to take away her love

I Ask the Darkness

My room is murky as my mind
The candle glimmers dimly
I ask the darkness
Why life meant
To be as winter grimly
I ask the darkness
Why God keeps
To take away my dearest
I ask the darkness
Why it froze my soul
And all my feelings

The Riddle

There is a message on the snow as a riddle
Please don't step on it and don't bypass
At night someone wrote furtively
"Forgive me darling" an assertive phrase
The blunder boiled in someone's soul
Who couldn't fight it any longer
Then sun will bring the morning glory
He pleaded for forgiveness in his story
Despite the chilly everlasting wait
He wrote this in hope to be noticed
It does not matter and there is no answer
If only she would read this and
Believe him one last time, no chances left
The message on the snow in bold letters
Words of repentance and regret
Escaped from heart, unable
To bear heavy burden of the guilt

Too Late

Silent morning devouring the dawn
Dreams are leaving and taking my vigour
Rigours of life during maddening war
No more captivating will send me ashore
Throw memories back as stones

Snow silently melting under the foot
I have no idea what happens
You're playing with feelings
Engaging the war, you are closing the door
It's too late to restore life of broken images

Foolish wind is biting the moon
Scatters stars in the sky as the pebbles
Let's keep silent for moment and hear the loon
You can see now how vanishing moon
Would accept me forever as sister

Conversation

I said to him: I love you, can't you see?
He brusquely replied: I'll take a look
I said to him: I'll die for you
He gave a look and smiled: It's up to you
I asked him: How I'll live without you?
He answered: Just fine, you'll forget me soon
I whispered: Let me prove
He said in disbelieve: Please don't delay
I went to window and plummeted in the darkness
In farewell I softly said: I love you
And then he felt his heart was pierced
By something new, inadvertently
He uttered words: Why do I need my pride?
He looked at silent darkness and
Then bawled: Why am I still alive?

One Day

You will marry a stranger
You will scarcely whisper "I do"
You will lie and reliance explode
You will throw your love in the bog
You will tighten loops of the rope
You will go to extreme and spare nothing
In ardour of this trivial war
Please be silent. You truly expecting
Me to wish you good luck on this day?
Wasted years slipped down unnoticed
In the bottomless pit as moray
You had sworn to protect me
That autumn but you made me a victim
Of the callous fight that I'll never forget
I'll never forgive the high price of mistake
As you called it "misfire" and torrential rains
Washed away love from ruins of life
Slow-motion shot: joyful bride and groom
As the movie and only I am missing the part
But invited for screening

Nostalgia

Half of your life was passed without me
And during a peaceful dinner
You'll shiver suddenly and drop the spoon
And conversation stops with awkward silence
You suddenly will leave the room and close the door
You'll take away my hidden pictures
You'll catch a breath and flood your heart
With emptiness and drilling pain
Caressing with the sight of my faded pictures
You will recall us running in the rain
For the umpteenth time you'll kiss that picture
And ask: what for the piercing pain?
The time is lousy doctor as you see
I won't be with you, I live in other country
There are no trains, or planes, or cars
You can't buy a ticket, you don't need a passport
It is easy to get there in your dream
The name of the country is Nostalgia
Your soul will tremble with excitement
You'll understand what you had missed
Then you'll put away my pictures and return for dinner
And see that food is cold and your wife is not pleased

Wedding Thoughts

Have any of you looked
Through the bridal veil
Have any of you stood
In front of an altar
And answered aloud: I do
Have any of you stared in the eyes
And noticed the question and grief
Have any of you caught by surprise
In front of heavens and earth realizing: it's pity
Have any of you threw a wedding bouquet
Into the crowd of desirous bridesmaids
Stricken by unacceptable thought
Better be dead than be here
Have any of you seen the bridal garland
The wreath of sacred worship
And thought: never-ending
Have any of you offered stone cold hand
To gaoler agree with unwitting
Have any of you dreamed of escape
From rigorous walls, disappear forever
Have any of you looked at wedding ring
In front of the altar saying: I do
And thought: I don't

Lonely

In front of mirror full of fraudulent pretence
I stood blindfolded - foolish bride in white
The taciturn voice of my
Timorously whispered words of love
Sufficing air with emotions
My hands were trying to catch a piece of sky
But you ignoring my entreats and vows
Clamped tightly and commanded: breathe
I fell from the firmament as a dying seagull
Strangled with your cruel love
And left forever deathless credo
You cannot live without love

I Asked the Boy

Tell me, are seagulls crying
When sea deceives them?
I asked the boy when sunny
Spring was breaking ice
And cheerful wind
Was happy playing
And boy had answered
When the sea betraying
Seagulls are crashing on the cliffs
Unable to keep living... they are dying

Bride

In white wedding gown
Anxious bride
By the window standing
Guests are here
But bride
Is unable to move
Hands are weak
Thoughtful sight
Is reflecting
From the window glass
Lips are stifling the shout
No means to forgive me
Lips are bleeding
Impossible pain
Breaking silence
But no one listens
Veil is slipping
She is dreaming of
Tearing off that doomed veil
And as if heard the bride's plea
Veil is falling to her feet
And she begins crying

Promise

You promised me the world
I asked you to be silent
You promised me all stars
I told you not to promise me too much
That pointless speech you gave
Expecting absolution would
Never help to cover your lies

Confession

My love, you had betrayed me
So many times, I've been so blind
To trust your promises and vows
You made a bet on love and lost the game
You traded my affection and devotion
For false impression, for mirage
The day will come; you'll pray to get embraced
By somebody but you are all alone
Insults and lies as bitter grimy wave
Will carry you to path of darkness
And words will burn your ears with pain
Do not complain, the punishment is starting

Don't Calm Me

Don't calm me, it's no longer needed
I made it up myself, the shooting stars
The crystal woe of otherworldly gems
The winter fettered soul, and yet again
I dream of fire enthralling and inviting
I never would disturb my heart
Let it unveil, better than to keep the silence

Don't calm me, it's no longer needed
The time is never turning back
The sky is black, look Milky Way
In tears and comets dropping like a rain
Forgive my sorrow and get ready to accept
The lonely life, the desolation
Are always loyal, never will betray
The heart that slowly turns to stone

The Ache

I am suffocating with anguish
With foolish, spiteful depression
The memory is taunting mind
Removing marks on gleaming road

He has betrayed and more than once
He will continue deceiving
The ache will wipe the brightness of the eyes
And grief rejoice ignoring poisoned tears

My love and twinge are always here
With me, united, twisted, uniformed
A burst of sorrow, regretting nothing
I'm drunk with grief, betray and forlorn

Rain in the City

It is raining again in my city
Streaming tears from heavens
You are not waiting for me
I am lingering for you
In the glow of brilliant fires
I descend to the emptiness
Through veils of nights
I hold out my hands
I will reach you, maybe
Gather my affection in palms
I will touch
Giving my heart away

Trembling Hand

The rain is pouring since morning
Until the autumn nightfall
The glum and bitter raindrops
Declared each other war
Over crossed out lines of my love
The angel is crying disconsolately

There is nothing left to return
Nothing to rescue
Not to hear a call, nor a word
And erasing the sign of my love
Heart is tumbling and
Singing with rain in unison

I needed some air, but can't inhale
And my eyes are burning from tears
Trembling hand is holding your letter
With two words: forget and forgive

Rain washes off fallen leaves so easily
Could it wash memories of you - I don't know
Lips are whispering: let me go
Set me free and don't torture

Silence is worse than the truth and the lie
Silence is conformably with hope
Rain whispering knowingly - if something returns
It will be never the same as before

Wind

The wistful wind is swaying branches of the trees
You are looking right through and ignoring me
I become deaf from heartrending cry
Wind came by silently and muttered: let's fly

Look at the sea coercing waves to shore
This is your love, not possible to measure
Where is reciprocity? Look at my eyes
End and forget, tear off your blinding net

I listen to the wind and watch sun sparking beams
Wind is right, I'm missing a stranger
What has he done to me?
It doesn't matter if only for a moment he loved me

The Autumn Is a Thief

Autumn stole you
Stole you without asking
Probably to play a joke
Kissed you under mighty oak
Moving as the gypsy dancing
Giving me the guilty glancing
Hexing, charming, stupefying
Trolls are helping, I'm flying
From the cliff, but I'll keep trying
Break the autumn spree of lying
Brewing potion of love
Autumn looked at me with pity
Saying: she is very pretty
Even for the holy city
Leave minacity and go
Join the friends and say hello
To the snow, think of us
As silver winter glow
As the dream that came from the past

Separation

What does it mean to be in separation?
It means the pain
The salt on never healing wounds
The tears of piercing expectations
The pain of tormenting ordeals

What does it mean to be in separation?
I was afraid of it
Forget the answers
Anticipate the sense
Still loving you

Don't Let Me Go

Don't let me go
Please follow my trail
As autumn foliage
Tunes of rains
Pour soul lavishly
Break down as
An inebriated butterfly
Die and revive but
Don't let me go

Nevertheless
I will turn back
Though shadow incorporeal
Of not subsisted love
I fill each step
Remember in my heart
Words of not sung songs
Are echoed by the cranes
And drifting farewell

The past - it wouldn't die
Gave everything
To time and torments
In unyielding captivity of love
Dreams bound
The separation takes
Its painful turn
And all I beg is
Don't let me go

The End

There was an early morning when you left
But seemed the night proceeded
You told me dryly: I am gone
We knew then I'm no longer needed
I kept the silence and on the wall
I wrote: my love defeated
The wall was cold as piece of ice
As snow slaps in blizzard
Dolour went through detaining heart
To tear apart my feelings
You didn't expect me to endure
The turpitude, the sneaky foul blow
I was not ready to accept
That you, my love, are implacable deceiver

You Left

You left and after that the sky descended
Immersing eerie wraithlike glow
Bestow weighty rumbling clouds
And raising so many doubts
Slowly confining my forbidden pass
You left. The strips of fog swung from the trees
From city wires, from the city lights
You left. And yet, I didn't even know
That I'll never outgrow the day you left

Forget About Me

Forget about me, put out of your mind
We've been together for too long
Let thunder break dark clouds above
Wild rain will wash away heart-rending traces
And help us to forget the taste of love

Forget about me, don't shed your needless tears
The words of explanations gone astray
We've lived too long side by side
In dreams' captivity, in city of illusions

Forget about me, don't promise anything
We've kept this conversation for too long
The words took off as midnight plane
And we were left at closed and empty gate

Set Me Free

Set me free, set me free
When tomorrow comes
I am not detainee
Your prisoner
Free and untying
The despicable knot
Of love
I am free
Winter is coming
Chaining boundless sea
Have a merit
I'll never be free

Forgive Me

Forgive me, my surpassing love
The end of phrase I swallowed at parting
Forgive for shiver in my lonely heart
And gentle whisper: we're departing

I won't approach you anymore
Incapable forget the contravention
Embittered future you
And devastating me

Forgive for my deceptive dreams
His promises and compromises
For desiccated lips without kiss
Last glance and never happened bliss

Farewell

I worshipped you
Then your parting
Petrifying words
Turned soul in the glass
You went away from me
Beckoned by distant star
You faded away as summer cloud
You left me for so many empty days
Made me believe
The end of time has come
The earth stopped spinning
The sun is dying, you took it all
What's left for me?
I have my pride, my saviour
And your horrifying "farewell"

Without You

It is hard to live without you
But to live with you is even harder
Time will elapse with rush
Thumb through my memories
Pursue anticipation
Look, hundreds of years have passed
We never meet again at last
Life crafting movie - we are cast
Of stupid comedy without ending
Perhaps desire willing to return
And I will banish all hopes swiftly
Maybe our new love flash
Will bring me back
O my, I am already dreaming

I Wouldn't

I wouldn't seek excuse to be close to you
I wouldn't look for you in alien crowd
I would abandon worn from love
My prayer wheel locked at ordeal and
Chained in inert steel and crowned with despair

I wouldn't dial your number during night
And your call would never break the silence
Maybe I get some sleep at starry night
Without fight, diluting in the love of smitten outsider

I wouldn't dream of you, don't worry anymore
I know everything precisely
The mourning ribbon intertwine concisely in my soul
I leave it in enticing shoal
As humble offer for the river gods

That Wasn't Love

That wasn't love, it didn't happen
But wounds in the soul are real and alive
The time stopped suddenly
The dream became a hopeless dispute
Like madness, like arctic summer
It never comes, it only will beckon
A fairy tale without ending in your eyes
I see the eerie light, my verve is broken
As always, you have won

It's Over

It's over and will not return
These dates which I waited and evaded
These thoughts proximity which frightened
And treasured hopes for days of love

Why so often we are not appreciating
To what we own and we wishing for
What others have we envy strangers
And feel sorry for ourselves

Without thinking simply losing
The fortune bounty, the priceless gift
Destroying bliss by own hand
Trying to pick up the pieces and
Build another castle on the sand

Mistake

We were together by mistake
The spring had passed and cherry blossoms shed
The feelings were impossible to keep
But wait, there weren't any feelings
Despite the fact it wasn't even sad
We've hardly been good friends, but lovers
We've met when we both looked for voyage
In land of passion and desire
We didn't care for the love
We wanted only to be pleased
We played undue and dicey game
Not thinking of the payment day
It came before we realized
And nothing can be fixed right now
The door to our past is now closed by mistake

Forever

I left you forever
You are near me no more
I will not leave a trace
Cover love with the ominous heavens
The kingdom of emptiness is ruling again
Quenches stars and tames runaway comets
I will plead for my love
Realizing it's already too late
And the love is forever forgotten
All these feelings and dreams
Broken, hated and lost
In a haze of dark lust
I left you forever
The pity of all
I left you forever
It was only *my* choice

Leave Everything Behind

Leave everything behind - the time without end
You will forget that seemed forever
The love will come, the love will disappear
The process is unending - this is a way of life

With glum you will recall the past
And you'll go on the road far, far away
Perhaps you will succeed or fail
It does not matter - leave it

Then you'll recall the times of yore
That lovely instance, the occasion
You'll force the smile and then get sad
Who said: leave everything behind... forever

Life Story

One day the girl was born
She grew, had expectations
She loved and worried
Then she vexed and lied
Lost all her peace of mind
She slandered, gambled
Spurred-of-the-moments
She prayed to God then
Sold herself to Evil
She cried and called him
Broke so many hearts
Comprised, defended
Waited, dreamed and grieved
Then sinned and argued
She laughed and danced
Then drove people crazy
She lived, grew old and
One day she died

Love Dies

Love dies not from ancient age
In quiet light of fading evening
Love dies from lassitude
From lies, from nonchalance, from dispassion

Love dies from indifference
And emptiness, and vanished colours
On canvas of the diurnal life
From taking "I love you" for granted

Love dies not from incurable disease
In company of grieving crowd
Love dies from careless mistakes
From anguish and neglected vows

If You Remember

If you remember me
I was alive that day
The dawn on my hair
Painted them golden
I smiled serenely
I spoke missing point
I looked at you
If you remember
The drops of amber
Flame of heartfelt fire
You do remember
I loved thee once
If you remember me

You Are Somewhere

I am alone
Talking to myself
You are somewhere
The dreams about
You leaving and ceasing
During night
You stopped to appear
In my thoughts
I lost a joy of flying
During night
My landing strip diminished
Becoming black without lights
I am alone here
You are somewhere

The Star

The star dropped from the velvet sky
Beckoned by mighty ocean
Before it vanished in abyss
Star prayed for love and everlasting bliss

The star's voice was shuddered
But echo saved its cherished words
And even ocean went silent
Hang over warning waves and foolish birds

The star asked heavens for forgiveness
Confessed in strange forbidden love
She spoke softly: I will perish
Condemned in passion, trapped with qualm

I was that fallen star, medieval witch
Burned on the hungry flame completely down
From grief, from sorrow and from anguish
My love, my life and odium are past

Letters

Forgive me for keeping your letters
I didn't burned them, didn't tear apart
As you requested, I couldn't force myself
To entrust your words to heartless fire

I recognized the grin of fortune in the fluster
Appreciated vanished time
I can't betray the minutes which
Once belonged to only us

The Love Is Gone

The love is gone and left a handful ashes
The burned feelings, charred phrase
The soul is sightless from seclusion
For what do I need the eyes if light is gone

The love is gone and left a knot of grime
The sea of sorrow, the ocean of deprivation
All questions senseless now as before
We'll never find the proper answers

The love is gone and left the empty frame
The blackened mirror, the ruins of sensation
We never thought what is ahead of us
A moment of refutation

The love is gone, it left without saying
Without trembling at tense back
Without giving hints, exchanging glances
Without chance to tell me: "I love you"

The Bay of Lost Love

My wings are broken and forsaken
I dropped my weapons to your feet
Not the humility made me to admit defeat
But vital bleeding and wounds of mistreat

But in captivity my spirit wasn't seized
The tears on face have stiffened
Not your insolence brought me those tears
But everlasting sun that's shielding me

Just let you know, wicked master
The azure autumn blooming aster
Will whisper answer to the philosophaster*
You'll never make me thrall

Departing life I dropped to your knees
As prostrate pray, the victim of the pointless slay
Today is time to give away... Please let me say
My soul will be Queen of hidden bay
The bay of our lost love

***Philosophaster* - a Latin satirical comedy by Robert Burton. Since the play is about someone who pretends to be a philosopher, the term itself has been used in more recent times to refer to a pretender to philosophy.

About the Author

Victoria Sedova is an accomplished author and literary translator. Her published works include one poetry collection, three academic books, three translated novels, and numerous articles and educational materials for schools, colleges, and universities. Her short stories and poetry have appeared in a variety of Canadian and international publications. She was born in Russia, grew up in Ukraine, and moved to Canada with her family in 1990s.

Victoria lives in Toronto, Ontario, where she continues to write and translate poetry, short stories, and novels. She is a member of the Literary Translators' Association of Canada and the American Translators Association.